When Someone You Love Dies

AN EXPLANATION OF DEATH FOR CHILDREN

Robert V. Dodd

ABINGDON PRESS
NASHVILLE

WHEN SOMEONE YOU LOVE DIES:
AN EXPLANATION OF DEATH FOR CHILDREN

Copyright © 1986 by Abingdon Press

ISBN 0-687-45025-X

The Bible quotations in this book unless otherwise indicated are from the Revised
Standard Version of the Bible, copyrighted 1946, 1952, 1971, 1973 by the Division of
Christian Education of the National Council of the Churches of Christ in the
U.S.A., and used by permission.

Bible verses marked *TLB* are taken from *The Living Bible*, copyright © 1971 by
Tyndale House Publishers, Wheaton, IL. Used by permission.

Cover art by Helen Caswell. Copyright © 1985 by Abingdon Press. Used by
permission.

98 99 00 01 02 03 04—17 16 15 14 13 12

MANUFACTURED IN THE UNITED STATES OF AMERICA

Contents

A Note to Parents

When I was eleven years old, my mother died. Even today as an adult I can still remember those emotions associated with her death. I will never forget the anger that no words could adequately express and the kind of hurt and pain that goes far deeper than physical wounds, but which is, nevertheless, just as real and potentially more harmful. There was regret concerning certain things that I had said and done, plus an equal amount of guilt concerning things that I had failed to say and do. The whole situation seemed unreal to me, and at first I tried to pretend that it wasn't really happening at all, or that it was just a bad dream and that very soon I would wake up and everything would be all right.

But, most of all I remember the sense of loneliness and isolation, which made me feel that I was the only child in the world who had ever lost his mother and that no one else could possibly understand how I felt or why. As the months and years passed, I was able to work through my grief, and the Lord worked a wonderful miracle of healing in my life. But it still seems to me that by and large, when there is a death in a family the children tend to be pushed aside or ignored. We are uncomfortable trying to explain death to children, especially when we are attempting to deal with our own grief. It is difficult for children to grasp the permanent effect of death upon the individual. In fact, it has been my observation that children under the age of five or six are not psychologically mature enough to fully comprehend the finality of death. They may seem to understand your explanation at the moment, but are likely to ask you several days or weeks later when the deceased will be coming home, or when they can see him or her again. The questions children may ask concerning death are often complex and sometimes seemingly irreverant, at least from an adult point of view. But because Christ Jesus blessed the little children and acknowledged them as a vital part of his kingdom, we must not ignore them, especially when they are hurting. Patience and a willingness to reaffirm both the reality of death and the hope of glory that Christ gives will eventually help children deal adequately with the subject.

With that in mind, I wrote *Helping Children Cope with Death* (Herald Press, 1984) to give guidance to adults so they can help children deal with the death of a friend or family member or their own anticipated death from a terminal illness.

*H*owever, *When Someone You Love Dies* has a different goal. It was written especially for children twelve years of age or younger, to help them understand what happens to them as well as to the deceased, when some significant person in their life dies. It will also serve to point the way for them to get the help they need to work through their grief. And *it is unapologetically written from a Christian perspective,* while seeking to maintain effective psychological insights that I have gained as a pastor and spiritual counselor. I hope it will help reassure them that they are not alone in their experience of grief and that their hurts can be healed.

This booklet is designed to be read either by or to children when a death occurs in the family or within one's circle of friends and acquaintances. Following that reading, the contents should be discussed with the children so that their questions may be answered. These brief pages certainly do not have all the answers and are not intended to anticipate every child's specific questions or needs. But the content should help encourage discussion with children about an often neglected subject.

May this work encourage you to help the children in your care when grief is shared by adult and child alike.

Robert V. Dodd

Introduction for Children

When someone you love dies, it hurts deep down inside in a way that is different from the way it hurts when you scrape your knee or cut your finger. But even though you cannot see the hurt with your eyes, the pain is just as real. This kind of hurt is called grief. A bandage or first-aid cream cannot help heal it. But there are some things you can do to make yourself feel better.

This book was written just for you, to help you know what happens and what to do when someone you love dies. Find a quiet place and read it by yourself or have an older person read it to you. Then, talk with that person about what you have read.

Do not be afraid to ask questions. Asking questions is how a person learns. Some questions may seem silly, and you may not feel like asking them. But, go ahead and ask them anyway. The person who gave you this book, or some other grown-up, will be glad to answer any questions that you may have. If that person cannot answer your questions, he or she will help you find someone who can.

The hurt called grief, which you are now feeling, may seem strange and frightening to you. But knowing that other people care about you will help make the hurt go away.

Why Does It Hurt So Much?

Why does it hurt so much when someone you love dies? It hurts because you are going to miss the company of the person who died. Saying that someone has died means that we will never see that person again in this life.

It hurts because we may wonder how we are going to live without him or her. If that person happened to be one of our parents, grandparents, a close friend, or someone else whom we need very much, it may seem as if life will never be the same.

It hurts because you may feel all alone and afraid, as if you have been left behind by the person who died. But, there are other people who understand how you feel and can help you.

It hurts because you may be wondering what will happen to you. If the person who died was someone who took care of you, such as your parents, then you will probably wonder how you are going to live without that person.

It hurts because all kinds of feelings are stirred up when someone you love dies. You may try to pretend that it did not really happen, or that the person who told you about the death was mistaken. You may feel like hitting someone or throwing something because the hurt makes you angry. You may try to blame someone else for the death even though that person had nothing to do with it. You may think that there is something that you could have done to keep the person from dying. You may feel sorry for something that you said or did. Or, you may wish that you had been more of a friend or helper to him or her.

Even grown-ups have feelings like these when someone they love dies. You are not alone in feeling the way you do. And you should remember that *there will come a time when you will be able to accept the fact that someone you love has died. Once you are able to do that, the hurt of grief will begin to be healed.*

Why Do People Act So Strange?

When someone you love dies, everyone who knew that person hurts in the same way you are hurting. Even grown-ups hurt when a close friend or family member dies. They may be angry, upset, or even cry. They may try to pretend that everything is all right when it is not. They may talk about things that do not really matter. They may offer advice that is not very helpful, or they may just sit quietly and stare at nothing.

They may not want to talk with you about the death, because they are trying to protect you from the hurt of grief. So, you may want to tell them that you are already hurting and that you want to know what is happening and why they are doing what they are doing.

When there is a death, certain decisions have to be made. A telephone call to the funeral home which takes care of the dead body needs to be made. The funeral service has to be planned. The casket in which the dead person's body is placed has to be chosen. Friends and family are called and told of the death. The grown-ups will talk with the funeral director and the pastor about some of these plans. Important papers will have to be signed. Even the clothes to be put on the dead person's body will have to be chosen.

You may or may not be involved in making these decisions, but you need to know about them so that you will understand what the grown-ups are doing.

When there is a death in the family, lots of people come to the home to let the family know how sorry they are to hear the sad news. Once these people arrive, they may not know what to say to your family or to you. So, they may do other things to let you know how much they care. They may give you a hug or a kiss, or just come and sit near you without saying anything at all. They may offer to play some kind of game with you, just to get your mind off this sad time. They may bring food or flowers or send cards. They are doing whatever they can to show love to you and your family during this very sad time in your lives.

Flowers remind everyone that life goes on and that the sadness and hurt will go away in time.

The food that is brought and the strength that it gives reminds us of the love and strength that our friends and family are sharing with us. And the cards are another way of saying, "I love you and I am sorry that you are feeling sad right now." In times like this it is good to know that people really do care about us.

What Happens When You Die?

When someone you love dies, you may wonder what happens to that person. Death is different from falling asleep or going on a trip. When you fall asleep, you wake up in a few hours. When you go on a trip, you choose to go. But you do not choose to die. And when you do die, you will not come back to your family and friends here on earth.

Death takes us away from those we love, even though we do not want to die or be taken away from them. The Bible calls death "the last enemy" that we have to face in this life.

If you ever go to a funeral, you may see the dead body of someone you know. You may notice that the person looks different. You are still able to recognize your loved one, but now the person does not look the same as when you last saw him or her. The person may seem to be sleeping, but if you touch the body, it will feel hard and cold like a wax figure in a museum. The face and hair do not look exactly the same either. This is because life has left the body.

The eyes no longer see. The ears no longer hear. The mouth no longer speaks or sings. The fingers no longer feel. The lungs no longer breathe and the heart no longer pumps blood. The brain no longer thinks. The body is dead because the life has been taken from it.

After the funeral the dead body is sealed in a casket and buried in the ground. But death is not the end of this story.

What About Heaven?

When someone you love dies, and that person was a Christian, death is not the end of his or her life. That special part of the person which made him or her alive, which you knew and loved, and which loved you, is no longer in the body. That special part of the person, which the Bible calls "the spirit" was taken from death to be with Jesus in heaven. Heaven is a place where Jesus, along with everyone who loves Jesus, will live together forever.

In heaven there is no death, no sadness, no tears, no hurt or pain. In heaven, people who love one another and who love Jesus will always be together. God, our heavenly Father, will be there along with all of the angels. Joy and laughter will take the place of sadness and tears.

When a person dies, he or she cannot live with us here on earth. And that makes us sad. But, because of Jesus that person can have life in heaven. That should make us glad. It helps us feel better to know that those loved ones who have died are in such a nice place because they trusted Jesus.

It should also make us feel good to know that because we love and trust Jesus, we will be taken away from death to live with him and our family and friends in heaven.

We cannot get to heaven by car or by train or by bus. An airplane or even a space ship cannot take us there. We can only get to heaven by loving and trusting Jesus to take us there. No one can explain exactly how he does it. But Christians believe that he takes us to heaven after we die. Death is real, but it is not the end, if we love and trust Jesus.

Why Did It Have to Happen?

When someone you love dies, you may ask, "Why did it have to happen?"

It happened because sooner or later all persons and all living things including plants and animals die. The big trees in your yard or those you see growing in the forests may live for hundreds of years, but they too will die. Bumblebees may live only for a few days after they are born. Then they also die because they are *living* creatures—like you and your loved ones.

People do not choose to die. They die because that is the way things are in our world. When their bodies are no longer able to live, they die. It may happen to young people or to old people. It may happen to the strong as well as to the weak. But death happens to everyone. Sickness and disease come. Violent crimes take place. Accidents happen, and bodies wear out.

We do not have to go around thinking about death all the time. A part of our growing up is understanding that sooner or later death will happen to all of us. But, we must also remember that for those who love and trust Jesus, there is still life in heaven.

What Happens at the Funeral?

When someone you love dies, a funeral service will probably be held.

The funeral is a service of worship held in a church, in a funeral home chapel that is like a church, or at the cemetery where the body is to be buried.

The purpose of the funeral is to give people a time to remember some of the good things about the person who has died. It also reminds everyone that the power of Jesus is greater than the power of death. What death has taken from us, Jesus will give back to us someday in heaven.

The prayers, Bible reading, and preaching at the funeral service let everyone know that even though the person who has died will be missed, we believe that he or she is with Jesus in heaven. That belief helps turn our sadness into gladness.

It is all right to cry at the funeral or whenever the tears come. Don't be ashamed of crying! It is nature's way of helping us cope with the loss of our loved one.

Sometimes, someone may cry with us. By sharing grief and tears together, we may feel closer to the spirit and love of our lost one.

Sometimes, our tears of sadness may be mixed with tears of joy. We may be sad that our mother, father, sister, or other close person is gone. But we may be glad that person is now out of pain and suffering if he or she was sick before death. That person is with Jesus—in heaven where there is no more suffering or sickness.

Where Can We Find Help?

When someone you love dies, you may need help to heal the hurt of grief that you feel inside. But where can that help be found?

You can go to Jesus in prayer. You can be alone in some quiet place and talk to him out loud, just as if he were right there in the room with you.

Jesus' spirit is with us even though we cannot see him with our eyes or touch him with our hands. We can tell Jesus exactly how we feel and know that he will always understand. Jesus is the best friend that we can ever have.

Jesus knows how it feels to lose a loved one in death. Jesus can help us heal the hurt that we feel. He helps us by putting good thoughts in our mind to make us feel better. Or he may tell us some other ways of getting help. He speaks to us by putting good and helpful thoughts in our minds.

You can read the Bible yourself or get someone else to read it to you. The Bible will tell you about God's love and the way Jesus can heal your hurt. It tells about heaven and what we need to do so we will be taken there after we die.

Here are some Bible verses that you may want to read or have someone read to you: Psalm 23:1-6; John 14:1-21; Romans 8:14-39; I Corinthians 15:3-57; Revelation 21:1-4; 22:1-5.

You can talk to some grown-ups about how you feel and ask them questions that you may want answered. A parent, grandparent, or older family member may be able to help. Your pastor, teacher, or school counselor will also be able to help you understand your feelings about death and answer your questions.

Do not give up. Keep looking and asking for help until you find the right person who can help you.

Will It Ever Stop Hurting?

When someone you love dies, you may sometimes wonder if it will ever stop hurting, or if life will ever again be the same.

You will always remember the person who died, but you will not always hurt when you remember. Things will never again be exactly the same as they were before, but they will be better than they are now.

You can be thankful for the good memories that you have about the person who died. You can remember the many good times you shared together.

You can be thankful for the family and friends who showed they care about you. You can be thankful for and recall the message of the Bible and the hope that Jesus gives us that death is not the end.

One day we will be with those we love in heaven. But,

right now Jesus wants us to go on living on earth and telling others about the love and hope he gives us. We can be thankful that someone told us about Jesus' love and that Jesus can help us heal the hurt of grief. We can go out and tell others that they do not have to hurt any longer. Jesus can heal the hurt in our lives, when someone we love dies. Jesus' friends will show us the way.

"And whoever lives and believes in me shall never die. Do you believe this?" (John 11:26)

"So keep on believing what you have been taught from the beginning. If you do, you will always be in close fellowship with both God the Father and his Son. And he himself has promised us this: eternal life."(John 2:24-25 TLB)

*A*dditional Reading

Helping Children Cope with Death by Robert V. Dodd (Herald Press, 1984) enables the reader to enter into the child's experience of confronting death and provides psychologically valid and theologically sound advice on how adults can be more helpful to children as they seek to work through their grief.